AF338293

Hogtown Hammers
1 2 3 4 5 6 7 8 9 10 R H E
VISITOR 00000000 000
HOME 00000000 000
AT BAT 00 BALL 0 STRIKE 0 OUT 0 H/E 0
No Seats Available

The Ninth Inning

Written By ZaZa

Illustrated by Dream Computers

Produced by MRPwebmedia

ZaZa
Books for Kids

HH
Hammers

The Ninth Inning

The day was hot;
the teams were cold.
No runs had crossed the plate.

GO HAMMERS!
GO HAMMERS!
GO HAMMERS

A nervous energy filled the air.
The fans were in a state.

Eight innings now
were in the books.
But nothing had been done.

BB
BEANVILLE BATFISH
H

The pitchers had been dominant.
The batters had no fun.

Hogtown Hammers
1 2 3 4 5 6 7 8 9 10 R H E
VISITOR 0 0 0 0 0 0 0 0 0 0 0
HOME 0 0 0 0 0 0 0 0 0
AT BAT 00 OUT 0 H/E0

O'Malley stood upon the mound.
The sweat poured down his face.
He brushed his hand across his brow
To remove the excess waste.

Caplinski strode towards the plate.
Determined to end the game.
His reputation was on the line.
The result would mark his fame.

HH
Hammers

The masked receiver
flashed his signs
With a semaphore's precision.

O'Malley nodded in agreement,
At his battery mate's decision.

BB

O'Malley began his pitcher's dance.
A contortion of practiced deception.

BEANVILLE BATFISH

But Caplinski just watched
the ball fly by,
Not liking its fight's direction.

"STRIKE ONE!"
cried the Ump.

But Caplinski just stared,
To register his objection.

The crowd grew wild
like a colicky child.
Their behavior
was not subtle or mild.

They screamed and they yelled
But the Ump held his ground,
Despite their demand for his hook.

But Caplinski stayed calm
And with a hero's aplomb,
He acknowledged
the Official's decision.

HH
Hammers

He raised his right hand
to quiet the crowd.
He grumbled of times gone by:
"This ain't no Casey at the bat,
No need to pout or cry."

Hammers

The fans grew silent.
The vendors stood still,
As they waited
for O'Malley's next pitch.

Hoping for one
that Caplinski would like.
Just one he could land in the ditch.

Hammers

O'Malley wound-up
and let the ball fly.
A knuckler as the bait.

BB

But Caplinski watched and waited,
As the ball danced across the plate.

“STRIKE TWO!”
cried the Ump.

The fans were all stunned,
As they saw the end drawing near.
But baseball differs
from ordinary games,
For an end is never quite clear.

HH
Hammers
Hammers

So Caplinski stayed alive
by fouling each pitch.

Till O'Malley began to sag.
The hope and the prayer
that permeated the air,
Was that O'Malley
would develop a glitch.

BB

On the twentieth try,
the ball started to die,
As it connected
with Caplinski's large bat.

The ball left the yard
with little regard
For the hole
that it made in the fence.

Hot Dogs!
Enjoy the taste
Hammers

The game was all done.
The fans had their fun.
And on this you can surely rely:
All will say they were there
when a burst in the air,
Came from Caplinski's
deciding home run.

Game Over!

The Ninth Inning

The day was hot; the teams were cold.

No runs had crossed the plate.

A nervous energy filled the air.

The fans were in a state.

Eight innings now were in the books.

But nothing had been done.

The pitchers had been dominant.

The batters had no fun.

O'Malley stood upon the mound.

The sweat poured down his face.

He brushed his hand across his brow

To remove the excess waste.

Caplinski strode towards the plate.

Determined to end the game.

His reputation was on the line.

The result would mark his fame.

The masked receiver flashed his signs

With a semaphore's precision.

O'Malley nodded in agreement,

At his battery mate's decision.

O'Malley began his pitcher's dance.

A contortion of practiced deception.

But Caplinski just watched the ball fly by,

Not liking its fight's direction.

"STRIKE ONE!" cried the Ump.

But Caplinski just stared,

To register his objection.

The crowd grew wild like a colicky child.

Their behavior was not subtle or mild.

They screamed and they yelled

But the Ump held his ground,

Despite their demand for his hook

But Caplinski stayed calm

And with a hero's aplomb,

He acknowledged the Official's decision.

He raised his right hand to quiet the crowd.

He grumbled of times gone by:

"This ain't no Casey at the bat,

No need to pout or cry."

The fans grew silent. The vendors stood still,

As they waited for O'Malley's next pitch.

Hoping for one that Caplinski would like.

Just one he could land in the ditch.

O'Malley wound-up and let the ball fly.

A knuckler as the bait.

But Caplinski watched and waited,

As the ball danced across the plate.

"STRIKE TWO!" cried the Ump.

The fans were all stunned,

As they saw the end drawing near.

But baseball differs from ordinary games,

For an end is never quite clear.

So Caplinski stayed alive by fouling each pitch.

Till O'Malley began to sag.

The hope and the prayer that permeated the air,

Was that O'Malley would develop a glitch.

On the twentieth try, the ball started to die,

As it connected with Caplinski's large bat.

The ball left the yard with little regard

For the hole that it made in the fence.

The game was all done. The fans had their fun.

And on this you can surely rely:

All will say they were there when a burst in the air,

Came from Caplinski's deciding home run.

Two Dragons Named Shoe
Written By ZaZa
Illustrated By Dream Computers
Produced by MRPwebmedia
ZaZa
Books for Kids

The Criminal McBride
Written by ZaZa
Illustrated by Dream Computers
Produced by MRPwebmedia
ZaZa
Books for Kids

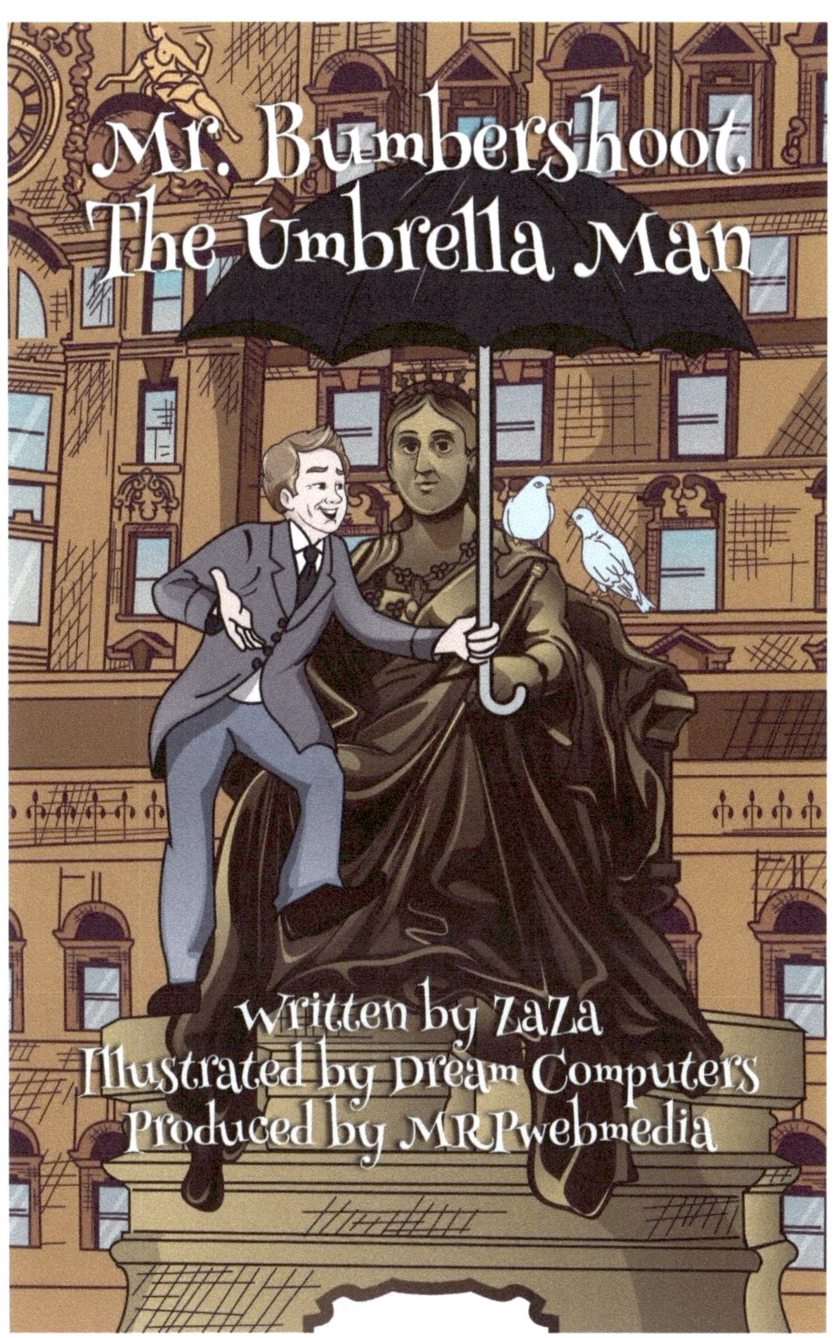

Mr. Bumbershoot
The Umbrella Man
Written by ZaZa
Illustrated by Dream Computers
Produced by MRPwebmedia